The Final Round:

Fight for Your Life

By: Tiera Gandy

Tiera Gandy

All Scripture references included in this book are from the King
James Version of the Bible.

ISBN-13:978-0692868706

ISBN-10:0692868704

Published by Tiera Gandy

DEDICATION

*I would like to dedicate this book to all of you
who have had the fight of your lives, or are
currently going through the fight of your life.
You're not alone, the fight is fixed!*

Table of Contents

For we wrestle not against flesh and blood but against principalities, against powers, against the rulers of the darkness of this world, against spiritual wickedness in high places.

-Ephesians 6:12 (KJV)

ACKNOWLEDGMENTS

I would like to acknowledge my family, my husband, Lance Gandy who has pushed me and encouraged me to finish this project, our children, Trey and Alandria Gandy.

I would also like to acknowledge my parents who have always been there for me and built a strong foundation of Christ in my life and my sisters and brothers who have been great role models for my life. And to my grandparents who have passed on and my grandmother who is still living, thank you for the foundation you provided.

To my friends, you all are amazing, thank you for believing in me and holding me accountable in finishing this project.

Introduction

Finally, my brethren, be strong in the Lord, and in the power of his might. Put on the whole armor of God that ye may be able to stand against the wiles of the devil. For we wrestle not against flesh and blood, but against principalities, against powers, against the rulers of the darkness of this world, against spiritual wickedness in high places. —Ephesians 6:10-13 (KJV)

What are you fighting for? It's simple, everybody is fighting for something. There are people in a mental prison fighting for freedom, couples fighting for their marriage and children fighting thoughts of suicide and self-harm. Everyone is fighting some sort of battle, but the real question is, are we fighting with the right weapons?

The Final Round: Fight for Your Life was created to guide you and to encourage you to stay in the fight, no matter how difficult life can become. It took me three years to write this book. I started it in the year 2014 and things changed from my idea to God's idea, this was a fight within itself. What I began writing in 2014 was not what God wanted me to complete. I started out with "The Unborn Woman", then on to "The Ultimate Battle" and finally God stepped in and said, "The Final Round: Fight for Your Life". Instantly it clicked.

My life has been composed of so many fights and struggles, like anyone else, but this book is my vehicle to tell my story the way God wanted it to be told. In my story I found that my fights were spiritual and I needed to learn how to fight them spiritually and not carnally.

If you don't know already, there is spiritual warfare around us. We struggle with opposition of the powers of the darkness, the enemies who are trying to keep us from God and from Heaven. We have a job to do. There's a fight coming, and we as a people need to be prepared. I began the introduction with Ephesians 6:10-13 because we have to know how to fight, how to be prepared to fight, who we are

3

fighting and what weapons to use:

Step 1:

Finally, my brethren, be strong in the Lord, and in the power of his might. -Ephesians 6:10 (KJV)

The Bible tells us to be strong in the Lord and in the power of his might. We have to be strong no matter what comes our way, strong in service, strong through our suffering and strong for fighting. Without God we are nothing, we are completely weak and will lose every fight if we don't cling to Him and dress for battle.

Step 2:

Put on the whole armor of God that ye may be able to

stand against the wiles of the devil. Ephesians 6:11 (KJV)

The full armor of God (Ephesians 6:14-18):

- Girt of Truth- A belt of Truth. Believers have God's truth.

- Breastplate of Righteousness- Satan attacks our hearts and our emotions; therefore take your breastplate of righteousness to guard your heart. The breastplate shelters your heart and prevents it from getting shot with arrows of wrath.

- Feet shod with the preparation of the gospel of peace- To adhere to the gospel and abide by it. Walk steady and upright and be a believer not just on the inside but on the outside as well.

- Shield of Faith- The most important! The shield of faith protects us from the devil and his fiery darts, temptation, etc. Satan is wicked and we use the shield of faith to prevent getting hit with the darts shot due to their swift and undiscerned flight. Never leave the house without it.

- The Helmet of Salvation- the helmet secures the head. This will purify the soul and keep satan away. The helmet will also keep Satan from troubling our minds. Salvation keeps us focused on God and keeps our hope in God.

- The word of God is the sword of the Spirit- the word of God is very necessary, satan knows the Bible just as well as the best scripture quoting Christian, but the difference is knowing the word for yourself and using it against him.

- Prayer must buckle on all the other parts of our Christian armour. We must join in prayer with all of these, for it is our defense against these spiritual enemies, with assistance from God. We must always pray for ourselves but especially for others. (prayers of confession of sin, thanksgiving, and petition of mercy, or just to speak to Him)

For we wrestle not against flesh and blood, but against principalities, against powers, against the rulers of the darkness of this world, against spiritual wickedness in high places. –Ephesians 6:12 (KJV)

Tiera Gandy

What is our danger? Who are we fighting? Our enemies are the devil and all the powers of darkness. The fight is not in the flesh but it is in the spirit realm, against several ranks of devils. I always say, when you overcome and graduate to another level, there are always next level devils awaiting you and they don't fight the same way as the last ones did. They come harder, sneakier and smoother than the ones before, pick up your shield of faith and guard your heart. It's time to FIGHT!

The enemy is powerful and numerous, vigorous and rule in the nations of darkness. They are spiritual wickedness in high places. Satan is a spirit, and our danger is greater from our enemies because they are unseen. So we have to adhere to the Holy Spirit and see with our spiritual eyes. This battle cannot be fought in the natural, or in the flesh, it must be fought in the spirit realm. It is said that the devil knows all God knows about your purpose and your life, past, present, and future. Therefore, all that God has prepared you for; the devil wants to keep you from pursuing it. Not just pursuing your purpose, but he wants your soul, he doesn't want you to go to heaven. Our duty is to put on the whole armor of God and to stand our ground. We have to stand up against the devil by God's grace and stand armed with the sword of the Spirit.

The Lord placed it on my heart to share my story and my testimony broken down into the fights I've had myself, and how I had to learn to fight my battles spiritually with the word of God and with prayer and fasting. God has taught me so much about what it means to be a believer, a true follower of Christ and I am here to extend that to you.

The Worldly Fight

Now the Spirit speaketh expressly, that in the latter times some shall depart from the faith, giving heed to seducing spirits, and doctrines of devils; -1 Timothy 4:1 (KJV)

There is a spiritual war going on in the world as we speak. So many people are blinded from it. Many people are falling away from the faith claiming that Jesus is not real and that he was made up, following as the scripture says doctrines of devils. Be careful to not fall into this category. Jesus is coming back and these are the signs that confirms it. Be watchful and get ready!

Sometimes we lose focus and that is okay, but

thank God for second chances. Repent and get back on the path to righteousness and stay focused.

Remember God has a purpose for your life; He created you and intends for you to live life in His will. Your purpose may open up the gates for someone else, which is why it is so important for you to find out what that purpose is.

What do you want to be remembered for? What will your legacy look like? These are some great questions to ask yourself as God continues to reveal His will to you.

Fighter, you have already won the victory! Jesus won that battle at the cross. He died so you and I could live and be forgiven!. That is what we call unconditional love. God does not care what you've been through or what mistakes you've made, all He wants is you. If you haven't already established a relationship with Him, I encourage you to pray and talk to Him and let Him turn you into who He has purposed you to be.

As you walk through my story and my life, please be aware that I didn't always have a strong relationship with Christ, I was rebellious, fearful, had low self-esteem and simply did not think I deserved to be alive. But as I grew closer to God and opened up to having a relationship with Him, I began defeating my inward battles.

I am not perfect, and my story isn't either, but I thank God for grace and for second, third, fourth, and one hundred chances, in my case. If God can use me then he most certainly can use you! Let's go!

Gloves on! Fight Time!

Get in the Ring

In boxing you fight in rounds. In order to progress to the next round in your life, you must overcome your current fight. Therefore you need the right attire, endurance, stamina, and the right combination!

It's time for you to get in the fight. The devil is not going to let you go easy. Training season is the most important part of your fight, what you do in practice is what will make or break you in the final round!

Training Season

Train up a child in the way he should go: and when he is old he will not depart from it. Proverbs 22:6 (KJV)

The foundation of my life started with my grandparents on both my mother and father's side. My parents were both raised in the church and were encouraged to carry that on with them from their childhood days to their adult lives. They did their parental duties and passed the baton to myself and my siblings to be stand up men and women of God.

My parents established a firm foundation when I was growing up. They made sure we were at church most Sundays; if we didn't make it to church we had a big breakfast and had church at home! My parents taught me to pray, to read my bible, to go to church and later to study the word in depth. My father has been the chairman of the steward board for years, while my mother has always been active in church and constantly takes notes during sermons. Growing up I watched her keep notes, and eventually, I began to take notes. I remember in middle school, I would invite my friends to church but always made sure I was taking notes, just like my mother did during service. I duplicated and imitated what my mother was doing and even now, I take notes faithfully during church and return to them when needed.

During your training season, you are creating habits and skills to prepare you for the fight. Your fight began when your mother became pregnant with you. God allowed for you to be born to fulfill your purpose in building His kingdom.

Being pregnant, I began praying over my son as soon as I knew he was inside of me, and I continued to pray throughout my entire pregnancy. During this season, begin praying for your purpose before God reveals it to you, for your spouse before God gives him/her to you, and for your children before God gives them to you. Execute your faith by training your mind to pray for and about any and everything.

Our minds are the root of everything we feel whether we feel happy, sad, insecure, love, anger, or loneliness, our minds absorb habits and thoughts like a sponge. This is why we have to protect our minds with the helmet of salvation and remember to guard our minds just as we guard our hearts. Every thought begins in your mind, and it is your responsibility to determine what kind of mindset you will have in this life.

Boxers train in certain areas for certain reasons; punching bags for power and endurance, speed bags for rhythm, foot work and weave game. Your weave game is important, you have to know when to duck and dodge your opponent.

What does that mean for us in training season in the spirit realm? It means that we have to train ourselves to be just as smooth and sleek in this fight spiritually and be able to discern when the devil is attacking us. This means you have to read the bible, study the bible, take notes, write down God's will as He reveals it to you, pray about everything, and give your life to God and be free from the world of sin. Remember, the devil knows the word, too. Stay guarded!

In the midst of the fight, you must know how to breathe through the rough times and the pain that comes along the way; it helps you to endure longer and to push through when you feel like giving up. Breathing in this case is equivalent to prayer. Prayer helps you remain calm and stable, just as breathing does. Our prayers to God help us communicate our needs to Him, in order to keep going, whatever it takes to help you not give up. Think about it, when you hold your breath, it makes you tense up and clench your fists. Therefore, not taking time to pray to God hinders you from going forward and experiencing all He has for you.

The devil will come at you with the wildest situations to make you desire to give up; to scare you out of your purpose; all I have to say is, don't let him.

The fights you've had within yourself, in relationships, friendships, family, and purpose are all a part of your story. They were set up for bad, but

19

became something beautiful. The devil wants you to quit fighting but God created a survivor in you. You can't quit!

We have to learn how to let the walls we build up become bridges for other people. Whatever or whoever hurt you and caused you to go through your rough situation should allow you to share your testimony with others, and allow it to become a bridge for them to come to Christ. Those pains are just war wounds which become scars. War wounds are there to remind you of the fight, not to keep you there. Be delivered! God is there to build you up and to strengthen you in those moments when you feel or have felt weak. Pray and spend time with Him so He can equip you and mold you into the man or woman of God, He has designed you to be.

Training season can be rough; you've got to prepare for the fight, be consistent and know your opponent. Remember where you started, remember how your faith even got to this point. No, we are not all at the same point in our faith, but we all started somewhere, and the good news is, one day we will finish, one day our stories will be complete. So, be fearless and jump in the ring!

Get your gloves on and get ready for each round, because he is going to come harder than he did before. As your faith increases, the fights get harder, but all you have to do is train well, and outlast your opponent. The ultimate goal is to stand with God's strength against the devil and his demons, and as long as you do your part in controlling your thoughts, protecting your heart, and believing with all your might, you have the victory!

As we go through the fights of my life, I pray that this touches your heart, I pray it encourages you and empowers you in your own life and helps you to get closer to our father in Heaven.

Welcome to the Final Round!

Round I:

Birthing Purpose

Before I formed thee in the belly, I knew thee; and before thou camest forth out of the womb I sanctified thee, and I ordained thee a prophet unto the nations. --Jeremiah 1:5 (KJV)

I was born on January 14, 1987 in Arlington, Texas to Mr. and Mrs. Thurman Miles. My father is a native of Oklahoma, the youngest of ten children and one of the smartest people I know. He's a historian and most definitely gave me my love for history as well. We both could get lost studying the bible and ancient times. The fabulous Elizabeth Miles, my mother, is a native of California and she is as fierce as she can be. She is so outgoing and confident in who she is and nobody can tell her different. I am truly blessed to have the parents God gifted to me.

I have two sisters and one brother. I am the youngest by eleven years. My mother was diagnosed with kidney disease and was known to not have any more children, but to the family's surprise, she came home and announced that she was pregnant. Naturally, the one who's been the baby for the past eleven years tells them to, "take it back", but I've heard rumors that it was more like, "kill it". They tease her all the time with this accusation. With my mother being very sick, there was the question if she or I would survive the pregnancy. BUT GOD! To God's glory, we made it! Talk about purpose!

A woman being pregnant with a baby is a lot like being pregnant with purpose. Being that I spent most of 2016 pregnant, I can attest to this in the natural and in the spirit realm. God has awarded me to be a mother and I could not be happier. My son was my purpose in my womb and as the scripture says, God knows even now what He has purposed my son to be before he even arrived. *(Jeremiah 29:11 (KJV))*

Just as a baby is planted in his/her mother's

womb, God has birthed something in you that has
been inside of you since before you were formed.
God has prepared for you to do something in this
world. You need only to search Him to find it.

My mother could have aborted me and given up
before the fight began, but she didn't. She decided to
fight for her health and for me. When God reveals
your purpose, it is something you will have to fight
for. You have to protect your purpose as if it's a new
born baby. During my son's early weeks and months,
we were very selective in who we would allow around
him, and we always made sure they washed their
hands before holding him. Be careful how you handle
your purpose. The ugly truth is, you cannot allow
everyone to be around you and your purpose, simply

because not everyone is supporting you.

Now faith is the substance of things hoped for, the evidence of things not seen. -Hebrews 11:1 (KJV)

You must have faith at least the size of a mustard seed in order to pursue purpose. My mother had faith and believed God for a miracle, and that's exactly what she got. Although I had a few complications, I made it.

God may have given you a vision to start a business, or ministry, but if you give up, you never know what kind of impact it could have had on the world.

In 2009 I was attending my family church and started getting more involved. I had a passion for youth and I was on the praise dance team. We grow up going to church because, that's what we were trained to do by our parents, but at this time I wanted to find Him for myself and praise Him because I truly had the desire to, and that I did.

Our leader at the time, Pastor Jerome B. Price, Sr., would often make me lead youth Sunday and sometimes even youth motivation, which was a quick three minute topic for youth; he surprised me during service to come do it, one time. I literally had two minutes to come up with a topic. Looking back at it now, it seems as if he was training me up to become who God intended for me to become. It almost feels like he already knew I was called, even before I did.

In January of 2010, he had a brain aneurism while out of town on church business. Pastor Price was like a second father to me. I wanted to be just like him. I shadowed him and tried very hard to model my character like his, because of his poise and honesty as a pastor. The aneurism hit my family and church family extremely hard, as we were all very close to him and each other.

In March of 2010, he was taken off of life support and passed away. This incident broke my heart, as I was thinking that he would come out of it and go back to being normal, but he didn't. The last time I saw him was in January right before the aneurism, I was following him around the church trying to ask him for permission to do a girls class for the youth, he turned around, pointed at me and said, "Tee, whatever it is that you want to do, you just gotta do it, I love you Tee, but you just gotta do it." That was it, that was all I had left of him. In my mind

I was trying to get permission to start this class, but what he was saying was, Tiera, there are no boundaries, and if you're going to do something, stop talking about it, stop asking for permission and JUST DO IT! So when he passed away, it was my mission to seek God and to figure out what my purpose in life would be. I did not want to die without fulfilling God's will for my life.

Sometimes drastic incidents have to occur in order for God to light a fire under us. Immediately I began seeking God for my purpose. I had gone through a lot of changes during that time. I was in college, working two jobs, and trying to figure out this God thing.

I sought out counsel from our current youth minister and his wife, who prayed with me and fasted with me to help me begin the process. It was right before resurrection Sunday, on Good Friday; and God released the first piece of my purpose while I was driving with my mentor and one of my favorite supervisors. God spoke three things into my ear, one being a youth minister, motivational speaker, and one other but I'd like to keep that to myself until it manifests. I fasted and prayed for three days before He revealed it to me. It may take longer for God to reveal your purpose to you, but be consistent and truly seek His face if you really want to know what God's plans are for your life.

The Process

Pregnancy is one of the most rewarding but also one of the most difficult things I've done in my life. A small seed planted in your womb affects your entire body, mentally, physically and emotionally. But it's God's way of trusting you to have a child and raise him or her which is the greatest gift he could have given us as women, to birth a human being.

The first trimester was one of the hardest for me. Although I didn't get sick often, I was more so nauseous all the time, and extremely exhausted. At times I felt like I was in the twilight zone as exhausted as I was, team no sleep for sure! This baby seed was taking over my body! The first trimester literally prepared my body for the rest of my pregnancy.

Spiritually, when God plants purpose in your womb, first of all, He's saying, "I created you for this,

I trust you with this." God trusts you with your purpose; He trusts you to build His kingdom. I thank God every day that He trusted my husband and I with our son to raise him to become the individual God has purposed him to be.

I have to admit, I was afraid at the beginning. What if I lose my baby? What if I don't go full term? But God shut those thoughts down when I went to Him in prayer. He instilled the confidence I needed to make it to the end. He was also so generous to give me some hints as to what the gender of the baby would be. Seek and you shall find!

But fighters, why are we so fearful of our purpose when God has already approved it? Why do we tense up and get scared and/or doubt God? Even when He has clearly shown us the vision, we still doubt Him. Protect your vision at all costs. You are not you without your vision. The devil creeps in and tries to scare us out of our purpose, but we can't let him. God is in control! Fighter, He is the planter. Planting the seed is simply just the beginning of birthing your purpose. Take pride that God chose you to carry it out. Don't be afraid!

Yes, there are birthing pains throughout the entire process, but God will sustain you through the early stages and all the pain and turmoil you've experienced or that is coming your way. All that you are going through in the first trimester is preparing you for all you will need at the end of the tunnel when it comes to the very last push.

The second trimester was by far the easiest

and best trimester in my experience. I had more energy, and not to mention I found out I was having a sweet baby boy. The Lord knew I needed a boy. Spiritually this may be the time period where God reveals your purpose in detail to you, the ins and outs of all you are supposed to do. God called me to many things, but in this season of being pregnant, He told me to focus on this book and this book only. As hard as this was, I had to be obedient and do as He told me. You have to play your role in birthing your purpose, and that role is so simple, but we tend to make it so complex. Your role is to be obedient, to be His servant, and to do exactly as he says do. Enjoy this time and prep for your delivery date, because it's coming whether you like it or not. God has use for you and time is running out so put down all the foolishness and let's push forward to walk in our purpose, today! The big show is coming!

The third trimester felt like the longest trimester. I was extremely exhausted and completely over being pregnant. I was impatient and could not wait for it to be over to see my beautiful baby and to get my body back. Doctors give us an estimated due date, but all in all the baby will come when God intends for him/her to come.

Spiritually God may not give us the exact due date, but He shows us visions and dreams of what we should prepare for. Sometimes we get impatient and try to put things in our own hands, but God is ultimately in charge. For example, my due date was December 23, 2016, I was so impatient and didn't want to wait on God, so I scheduled to be induced on December 22, 2016. Well, show God your plans and He will show you His. Trey Allen Gandy came on December 21, 2016 at 8:16pm, meaning I went into labor on December 20, 2016. God said December 21, 2016 for my little one and I thank Him for giving me such a handsome healthy little boy!

My plan was not to get a cesarean section (c-section) but due to complications, I could not escape it. My husband and doctor both knew how much I did not want to have a c-section, but there was nothing I could do, the important thing was having both me and my son come out healthy. But I thank God for showing me up and illustrating to me that He is in charge, and everything goes according to His will and not mine. In the midst of your purpose, understand that things won't always go the way you planned, they almost never will, but keep in mind that God is in control, and as long as you remain obedient to His will for your life, you can't go wrong.

As God is getting ready to reveal your due date, don't forget your role. The closer you get to God and your purpose, the more the devil will attack you. So don't expect it to be all peaches and cream; if there's a struggle, you're on the right path. Fight for your purpose through fasting and praying, you have authority over your enemies. *(Luke 10:19 (KJV))*

The Fight

For the flesh lusteth against the Spirit, and the Spirit against the flesh: and these are contrary the one to the other: so that ye cannot do the things that ye would. -Galatians 5:17

(KJV)

The flesh desires what is contrary to the Spirit; the flesh wants the opposite of what the Spirit wants. This forms a fight in the spirit realm. Please do not be afraid of these things happening. When you have a spiritual fight, the devil is fighting you because you have something that he wants. He wants to deter you and distract you from anything that has your focus on God. My very first spiritual fight was a little scary for me, but God helped me through it to understand it and to know it would not be the last spiritual attack.

I was about twenty-three (23) years old, and was at home taking a nap and had a dream. As I opened my eyes, I tried to get up and was being held down, but there was nothing there, in the natural. I attempted three times to get up, and still nothing. The Holy Spirit told me to say the name of Jesus and it would release. That is exactly what I did and it was released.

Submit yourselves therefore to God. Resist the devil, and he will flee from you. -James 4:7 (KJV)

As I grew spiritually, I learned more about the devil and his schemes. I have learned that while birthing your purpose, you must cling to God and call onto Him through the transition, because you will be attacked, but the good news is that God has already won our battles. We must give everything to Him and let Him take control of our lives and fight our battles for us.

"Don't allow the devil to paralyze you from walking into your destiny." –Tiera Gandy

Score

Devil- 0

God-1

Tiera Gandy

Prayer

Heavenly Father, I ask that you would cover this fighter who's searching for purpose and/or who has found their purpose and are struggling to submit to you. I ask that you would guide him/her and push them into their purpose. Lord we know that timing is everything and we know our days and months are like minutes and hours to you. We just ask that you would help us to be patient in birthing our purpose and to look to you for guidance. Allow us to be deaf to the devil's words and schemes, and to only hear Your voice, O' Lord. We love you, Lord, we lift you up, praise you and adore you,

In Jesus' Name,

Amen.

Do you feel God has revealed your purpose to you? If so, how? What does he want you to do?

_____

_____

_____

_____

_____

_____

_____

_____

_____

_____

_____

_____

_____

_____

Tiera Gandy

_____

_____

_____

_____

_____

_____

_____

_____

_____

_____

_____

_____

_____

Round II:

Unspoken Words

[43] And a woman having an issue of blood twelve years, which had spent all her living upon physicians, neither could be healed of any, - Luke 8:43 (KJV)

Tiera Gandy

The woman with the issue of blood; what was her name? Why wasn't her name in the Bible? The focus was not on who she was but the focus was on her issue. This woman had a constant flow of blood. This is significant because back then, women who were bleeding were considered unclean. She had suffered with this disease for twelve (12) years. She heard Jesus was coming and made her way to go see Him. She did not allow her circumstance to deter her from getting to Jesus.

She believed that she could be healed if she could get to Him. Her hope was to simply touch his garment, so she could experience a healing nobody else could give her. Her faith is what pushed her through.

The back story is, Jesus was actually on his way to see Jairus' twelve (12) year old daughter who was presumed dead. His purpose for this particular journey was for the twelve (12) year old girl, not the woman with the issue, but was only passing through, when the woman found him. But that did not stop her. You see, she had gone to see every physician she could think of. The Bible says she spent her living on trying to find a cure, but when the physicians could not heal her, they measured her as incurable. This woman went to any and everybody except Jesus to get help and none of them could help her.

Sometimes instead of taking our issues to God, we take them to everyone else. We call our friends and family to talk about our "issues", but don't go to God until He's our last resort, and the funny thing is He still loves us. Twelve years she suffered. There are also times when God allows us to endure some issues for a longer season than others, simply so He can get the glory in the end.

The woman was determined to get to Jesus. There was a crowd around him, pressed up against him. I imagine she had to crawl on the ground in order to just touch Him. Her goal was not to speak to Him or for Him to even see her, but only to touch the hem of his garment. As she fastened her hands to his garment, she was immediately healed. This constant flow of blood, which she had for twelve (12) years had stopped.

Jesus felt power depart from him and he turned asking who touched him. His disciples were like, really Jesus, all these people and you want to know who touched you?! The woman was terrified and trembling but with strength and courage, she bowed at his feet and told Jesus all about her issue and he told her because of her faith, she was healed and to go in peace.

We have to have that kind of faith, boldness, desire, and courage to get to Jesus. He is waiting on you to come to Him. This woman may have been in pain, maybe she was talked about, either way she did not let her environment hinder her. Be encouraged fighter, you've got to fight through the crowd and get to your healer. I can imagine the peace she had simply because Jesus said she was healed. We are in control of how quickly we want to heal. I say that because, in order to begin the steps of healing all we have to do is take it to Jesus. But our problem is, that we want to hold on to our issues, when Jesus died so we didn't have to. Our healing can be so easy if we simply just take it to Him in prayer and take the necessary steps of letting it go. I identify with the woman with the issue of blood because I had my own constant issue in my life.

Ultimately, there are obstacles that come unexpectedly and some of those become inward fights that eventually push us to a place of darkness. Because I've tried so hard to block this incident out of my mind, pretending for years that it never happened, it wasn't until I was twenty-three years old shortly after I began searching for my purpose that this incident started haunting me. I began to have dreams and flashbacks about it. Sometimes I would question myself on whether it happened or not.

I was eleven years old playing with some friends, being the true tomboy I had always been. My two guy friends asked if I wanted to come to one of their houses to play a board game with them. I said that I would need to get permission from my parents first, which I did. It was okay as long as my friend's dad was there, which he was. I rushed back went inside, sat down at the table and a few minutes later, his dad came out of his room and said he was going to run to the store and asked if we wanted anything. We all said no, and at that moment, I knew I needed to leave, but I waited two minutes too late. His dad was in the car backing out when I finally said,

"Maybe I should come back when he gets back." Immediately they grabbed me, picked me up, took me to a room nearby and sexually assaulted me. I cried,

screamed, yelled, hit, but could not break free. They held me down, and that was it; the very moment I lost my identity.

That was the beginning of a lot of self-hatred. I felt as if it was my fault for a very long time. I held this in for twelve years. This was my issue. Those twelve years were years of self-destruction, I became a cutter, suicidal, and emotionally and mentally unstable.

I, like the woman with the issue of blood, was looking everywhere for someone to heal me, but I could not be healed until I got to the source. It took me 12 years to get there. But I got there. I didn't know who I was because I hadn't addressed all parts of me, the bad stuff included. But finally, I was ready and God allowed me to be ready. As I became stronger in the Lord, I believed He could and would heal me if I took my issue to Him.

Nobody was hindering me from getting to Jesus. My crowd was my own demons I was fighting in my head. The devil would try to convince me that the world would be better without me; that my parents would be happier if I was never born. He'd tell me that I wasn't enough and I believed him. I had to break free of my inner thoughts and the negativity the devil was whispering in my ear. I had to overcome ME.

I had to forgive two people whom I believed were my friends and whom had never apologized to me for what they did. I felt as if I had no control over myself and I never wanted to feel that way again. But just like the woman with the issue of blood, I had to get to Jesus. His power is so strong and so powerful that the call of His name will heal you inside out. No matter the pain you are experiencing or have experienced before, getting to Jesus is all you have to do.

As life went on, I started paying more attention in church my eighth-grade year and focused on God. My parents got me a teen bible, and I began to read it at school with one of my very close friends. Unfortunately, I would still cut because, in a very awkward way, it made me feel better. I was a perfectionist, and if I made a mistake or came up short, I would punish myself. I was not a loner, I had many friends and from the outside looking in seemed to be as normal as everyone else, but the truth of the matter is, I wasn't. You never know what a person is going through. I struggled to have confidence in being who I was, in sports and in relationships. Although my grades never reflected how I felt, I still had this emptiness inside.

One day I was at home, and I had an extremely bad day at school; my mom came home yelling at me about a chore I didn't finish, and that was the day I gave up. I had enough. I went to get a knife, went to my room, sat in front of the mirror and attempted three times to kill myself, but the last time my mother walked in. She screamed,

"What are you doing?!"

She got off the phone and made me sit down and talk to her, tears in her eyes, and asked me why. The first thing I said was you don't love me. My mother and I talked that day, and she explained to me that she loved me very much, I expressed to her how I felt but still never told her I was sexually assaulted, the only thing I focused on was that I didn't love myself. We had a great conversation, and that held me together for years to come. We established a better relationship, as mother and daughter we still had our moments, but my mother became my miracle, just as she said I was hers when I came into this world. A mother's love is the most unconditional love and the closest you can get to God's love.

Suicide is real and it is a sickness. If you've never had those kinds of thoughts or feelings, then you will never know how it truly feels to be that deep in depression where you feel and believe in your heart that the world would be better off without you. But if you have had suicidal thoughts, understand that you can and will overcome this sickness and time of pain. Killing yourself will not solve your problems, and it will never make your family and friends feel relieved that you're gone. That is a lie the devil tells us in our ear at our lowest moments. God is forgiving, and so are your loved ones. We will all make mistakes, but if we truly love each other the way God tells us to, then we will learn to forgive one another and help each other get to the next level, where ever we are.

The Fight

During this time in my life the devil was trying to take me out. He was trying to end my life because, he knew what my future held. He knew that God called me to write this book and every other endeavor to build His kingdom, and the devil does not want me or you to succeed. He knows that if he can get in our heads and play countless tricks on us that we will give up and lose. But God covered me in my twelve (12) year issue and he will cover you.

For some reason my mother came to my room door, (even if she doesn't know why) and busted in when she would always knock. If that wasn't God, I don't know what is. But I praise Him today because she decided to come to my room! She saved my life!

The spiritual fight I had in my adolescent years had to happen, so I could walk into my destiny. I had to cut so I could help other cutters.

For example, when I worked at a junior high

school, I was the site supervisor for a before and after school program. One of my staff members informed me that she saw cuts on a student's arm. So I pulled the student aside and talked to her. I told her to show me her arm and she did, but told me she had left her plate on her bed and the fork scratched her. She was obviously lying and looked at me dead in my eyes and told me that I could not I save her. I immediately prayed, in my head, because I saw the spirit in her that was rebellious and ungodly. I informed her that I would not leave her alone until I helped her. I called her mother and spoke to her and her mother was surprised and hurt, but we took the correct precautions to help this young lady. She got counseling and spent afternoons with me expressing herself and she eventually stopped. She just wanted to know someone cared. Later she'd informed me that her group of friends were cutters, boys included and she wanted them to stop, like she had. She wanted them to get help and even asked me to talk to them, but they never came. I still think about those kids and whether or not they got help, I notified the counselors, but did not know what happened after that. Because I had been a cutter and made up dumb lies about my scars, I was able to help this girl stop and I am so grateful God allowed me to help her. I also had to come close to committing suicide, so I could help others, and last but not least, I had to be sexually assaulted so I could help other girls overcome that demon. The first time I told my story about being sexually assaulted was at the school. God pushed me to tell them; but the outcome was unexpected. At least six of those girls had been molested or sexually assaulted. The worst part about it is all of them had told their mom or guardian, whom either blamed them for it or didn't believe them at all.

Therefore, at that moment I realized that I had to go through these spiritual fights and overcome so I could use my pain as my purpose, which then became my passion. I had to build a bridge for them to cross over and begin their healing. I became passionate about young girls. Just like that God added to my purpose. God allowed these things to happen to me because He knew what kind of future I would have. I am certain that during this time, my parents were praying for me, they came through and we beat the devil again--through prayer! We overcome because God uses the good and the bad for our greatness; He's intentional in all He does for us in our lives. He could have stopped it at any time, but God knew He'd get the glory out of me. And that He did!

Your pain is necessary for your purpose. You are an amazing person and God has allowed you to go through what you went through so you can someday help someone else. Your purpose and your gift are not for you, God gave it to you to help other people. My unspoken words were meant to not only kill me physically, spiritually, mentally and emotionally, but it was meant to kill my dreams and my future, and the vision God ordained for my life. If it were up to the devil and his demons, the girls God placed in my path would have never met me.

The devil wants to distract you from what really matters. I had to pull myself out of a pit after being stuck in it for twelve years. That pit of self-destruction prepared me for many upcoming pits, but it made it easier to overcome the fights I endured later, and through my issue I remembered that God was fighting right by my side! I use my testimony as a weapon against the darkness, no matter what, the devil does not win!

Score

Devil- 0

God- 2

Tiera Gandy

Prayer

Heavenly Father, thank you for your unconditional love! Thank you for the unexpected obstacles placed in our lives. We know that they have to occur in order for us to grow, Lord. I ask that you would cover this fighter in any unspoken words he/she may have and I ask that you would help him or her overcome their past obstacles and the ones ahead. Prepare them for what's coming next, Lord. I ask that you would keep him/her from paying attention to the distractions; rid them of them right now, Lord! I ask that you would help them understand that whatever happened to him or her, is okay, and they don't have to hide anymore. I ask that you would help him/her release their pain to You, Lord, not being afraid but feeling completely comfortable and free in doing so. We ask these things in your name, heavenly Father!

In Jesus' Name,

Amen.

Is there anything you've held in for years that you need to release and begin healing? Explain, go to God in prayer and begin the healing process.

_____

_____

_____

_____

_____

_____

_____

_____

_____

_____

_____

_____

65

Tiera Gandy

_____

_____

_____

_____

_____

_____

_____

_____

_____

_____

_____

_____

_____

Round III:

Unborn Era

Even when we were dead in sins, hath quickened us together with Christ, (by grace ye are saved;) (KJV)

Tiera Gandy

The unborn era of my life is my life before Christ. Sure I have been in church my entire life, but Christ was not embedded in me. Not that I didn't believe, but my life was not centered around Him. There was a time that I just existed and lived life the way I wanted to live it. These times included ungodly relationships, a lot of alcohol and clubbing, this was my life in college!

Eventually the pain I had endured as a child had become blocked out memories, as if the incidents never occurred. I acted as if I never had a problem with self-esteem, I did not deal with the pain, I suppressed it. I went on and had a great last (two) 2 years of high school and after graduation straight to college. I had a great freshmen year of college but returned home after becoming pregnant and losing a baby.

I started going back to church and began to get involved, before the "birthing my purpose" era of my life. At this time I was going out partying with friends and having a few drinks from time to time. To be completely honest, I was straddling the fence. Although I was involved at church I was still living life my way.

I would go to church on Wednesday, lead youth church on Sunday, but would go out on Friday and Saturday with friends, dancing and drinking. I even got crafty and stopped going out on Saturday nights and only went out on Friday nights with friends. I thank God that He covered me and my friends when we needed it most. There are two incidents that occurred in my life that were the most significant, and

I'd like to share them with you.

One of my close friends got extremely intoxicated that we had to call the ambulance and take her to the hospital. Everyone stayed at my apartment once we made it back. I was asleep and my friends and college roommate were trying to wake me up. I was completely knocked out, and my roommate literally had to slap me for me to wake up. They told me that our friend was so heavily intoxicated that they didn't know what to do. I got up and as she was lying in my lap, her eyes were rolling back, begging us to help her. I began crying but knew we had to do something; we called the ambulance, called her dad and rushed her to the hospital. She had to get her stomach pumped but made it through. The paramedics were glad we called and didn't wait until it was too late. We were unaware that she had began drinking before she came over to go out with us.

That day, my life and perspective on drinking changed, completely. I wanted to be more responsible, because that situation was too close to home for me. God again, showed up even when we didn't deserve it and I am forever grateful that she's still dancing around here these days. Going out to clubs and drinking at the time was fun; but I was trying to fill a void of unhappiness, insecurity, anger, and loneliness, due to broken relationships. But the void was only filled temporarily and when I woke up, not only did I have a hangover, but I still felt the same. Some of you may be doing the same thing, but let me tell you, it is not worth it. Intake of a large amount of alcohol can attack you physically, mentally and spirituality; just like that you allow spirits to come in and overtake your body, causing you to do and say things you may not have done or said if you were sober. Be very careful if/when you consume alcohol and please watch over your friends and family as well.

The second encounter I'm about to tell you about took the cake, for sure. I was out with a friend and at this time I had a two (2) drink rule, for myself. At this point had only one drink. A man asked if he could buy me a drink and I said yes, but I didn't check him, like I normally would. He handed me my drink with his hands on top of the cup, it was a long island ice tea. I took a few sips and immediately I felt as if it had a weird taste. Sure enough, not too long after, I began to feel out of control, I could barely walk and I know I was not highly intoxicated or drunk. I remember walking to valet hearing someone behind me saying, Oh they aren't going home. And I remember yelling, YES, we are! We left and I passed out in the car that night, like she thought I was dead, passed out. I made it home, thank God, but the next day I could not move. I was laying in my bed, pretty much paralyzed-like, until about 1:30pm. Finally I was able to move and ran to the bathroom and threw up. My best friend came over along with the friend I went out with and they brought me food and Gatorade and I felt much better but my face was broken out and I felt horrible. I did a little research and found out someone slipped a "mickey" date rape drug into my drink.

It is prominent that you stay guarded at all times

when out with friends drinking or not. I can't help but think God was trying to get my attention. Anything could have happened that night, but I praise and thank God that nothing did. I learned my lesson quickly after that and took a break from that lifestyle. Because of this story, I am able to tell the girls in my organization and other teens in order to prevent the same thing from happening to them.

Relationships were also hard for me in my life before Christ. It was because of the broken relationships that I would go out with friends to get my mind off of things, again filling a void. I had to get to a place where I didn't wallow on situations when people would hurt me. I had to move on and look ahead. Please know that nothing is going on that good in the past, so we have to keep pushing forward. Take a glance here and there to remember where you came from, but don't stay there.

The Fight

Through all of this, I simply had my times having fun, then I saw someone close to me go through something that could have ended her life and even went through something myself. After not healing properly, I turned to alcohol and somewhere I got lost. I found myself adding on to the previous pain I had in my last relationship, and searching for love in people unworthy, simply searching for something to fill a void.

Some of you are in relationships or "talking to someone" just because you don't want to be alone. You don't even like the person you're with; if that's you, you need to let it go and move forward, BY YOURSELF. There was a time when I didn't feel comfortable being alone, so I would go on dates aimlessly, not really looking to be in a relationship, but more so just company, nothing wrong with that, but you have to figure out who you are.

My college roommate and I began to do bible studies, and grew stronger in the Lord. She was my best friend, and accountability partner, most of all we understood eachother. We shed many tears together in our growth in the Lord. We built a great bible study class each Wednesday, not realizing this was the first tug that God was calling me, but I didn't even recognize it. Don't be like me and not recognize the first call from God, because you're so wrapped up in earthly things. Obedience is your best friend, if God calls, answer!

All in all, through college, I ran into a few bumps in the road, I was stalked twice and followed by one of them, humiliated on social media by the other. I dated guys who were out of my character, and I would go out drinking, just to make myself feel better and soon, I hit rock bottom! I didn't know how to fill the void and heal at the same time. Although I cut down on going out and drinking, it didn't count it out that I was still doing it. I was trying to find something in someone to help me be made whole, and I couldn't find it. Little did I know, I couldn't find it because there is no person on this earth who can fill a void of me being alone. The only one who could do this was God.

I was the person who had to hit rock bottom

over and over again in order to get back where God needed me to be. But that does not have to be you. I would literally hit rock bottom, climb out the pit, dust myself off and start over, but sometimes it seemed as if I jumped back into the pit, willingly.

God allowed me to experience so much pain but He informed me that sometimes it wasn't necessarily the devil, sometimes it was me. Oh yes, we love to blame the devil for everything but sometimes, it's just us. I was completely self-inflicting myself, spiritually, mentally and emotionally, but this time I wasn't cutting, it was an emotional abuse. I did things my way, and suffered in relationships because of it.

It wasn't until 2010 that I really began to work

on myself. I separated myself and went on a dating fast and for that summer, I hung with my girls and had the time of my life. I began to reflect on myself and figure out who I wanted to be and the kind of woman I wanted to be for God. I graduated from college, got a job and a house, and was living a great life. I took myself out on dates and spent time with myself, by myself! God was my king in shining armor, He won me over!

Fighter, if you are single and not married, I want you to know that you need not worry about your future. God has everything you need. If you need help detaching from a relationship, here are a few things I advise you to do.

Pray and ask God for guidance. My sister taught me this prayer to me: Lord, if this is not the person you have for me, please help me to let him/her go.

Seems so simple, but I promise it works.

Draw closer to God. Study His word and focus on what He is trying to teach you in your season of singleness. Allow yourself to be vulnerable and open with God, find a secret place to pray and worship Him and watch Him heal your heart better than anything you could imagine. He will instill strength in you mentally, physically and emotionally.

Forgive. Peter asked Jesus how many times he should forgive his brother; Jesus answered seventy times seven. (Matthew 18:21-22 (KJV)) Forgiveness is not for the person who harmed you or hurt you, but forgiveness is for you. God gives us grace and forgives us for our wrong doing every day, we should give others the same mercy. Forgive!

Make yourself busy. Get your smart phones out, go to your calendar app, and start your schedule. As a life coach, I do this anyway, because it helps me stay organized. Schedule your days and do some things by yourself that will get your mind off the breakup. Turn away from things such as alcohol and going out. You need to fast from certain things to clear your head. Go to the zoo, pick up a new habit, for example, join a boot camp or fitness class, exercising always relieves stress.

Take Your Time. If you were in a relationship for two years, take two months to fully heal. No talking to your ex-boyfriend or girlfriend or anyone else. NO REBOUNDS!

Be Ready. Stay alert! Once you are fully healed, go

on a date and do not allow the person who hurt you before to have control over you. When I say that, I mean, let your guard down. Give the next person a fair chance, with no baggage. Just because you were hurt before does not mean, this person will hurt you again.

Abstain from sex. True healing is when you can abstain from sex. It is possible, even though in our world, today it seems impossible. When we as humans have sex with one another, our souls join and every person you have sex with becomes a part of you.

Don't get me wrong, sex is a good thing. God created sex to be something good but between a married man and woman. That's it.

Pray for God to strengthen you in this area if needed.

Last but not least, purpose search. Add purpose search. When God sends your spouse and you start a family, your time will be limited as to how much time you will allot to your purpose. I'm not saying it cannot be done, but it takes a lot of sacrificing. While you're single, the Lord advises you to focus on Him:

But I would have you without carefulness. He that is unmarried careth for the things that belong to the Lord, how he may please the Lord: But he that is married careth for the things that are of the world, how he may please his wife.

-1 Corinthians 7:32-33

If you are currently single, begin praying for your future spouse now and let God work on him or her.

Ask God to help him or her be a Godly individual who puts God first in his/her life. Do not rush into getting married, simply because you don't want to be alone. The worst thing you can do is settle for someone who is not ready for marriage, which in fact is losing before the fight even begins. Allow God to write your love story and give Him complete control of all areas of your life.

Score

Devil-0

God-3

<u>Prayer</u>

God, I ask that you would touch the person reading this who may have suffered from broken relationships and/or is currently going through a rough time trying to fill their voids with drugs, sex, alcohol, meaningless relationships, or whatever their struggle may be. Help them to be strengthened to let go of the things that are not like You; break the chains O' Lord, restore them with the Holy Spirit and help them to live in FREEDOM with You! Help them find what they desire in you, peace, love, joy, and happiness! We know this CAN be done if we just trust you, Lord, we love you, we praise you and we lift you up!

In Jesus' Name,

Amen.

Tiera Gandy

What does your life before Christ look like? How can you move forward from it? What steps do you need to take?

_____

_____

_____

_____

_____

_____

_____

_____

_____

_____

_____

The Final Round: Fight for Your Life

_____

_____

_____

_____

_____

_____

_____

_____

_____

_____

_____

_____

_____

_____

Have you healed from all past relationships?
(Friendships/Family, included) If not, what
relationships do you need to heal and why? What
steps do you need to take in order to heal
wholeheartedly?

_____

_____

_____

_____

_____

_____

_____

_____

_____

_____

_____

_____

_____

_____

_____

_____

_____

_____

_____

_____

_____

_____

_____

_____

_____

Round IV :

Know Your Opponent

Moreover the word of the Lord came unto me, saying, Son of man, take up a lamentation upon the king of Tyre, and say unto him, Thus saith the Lord God; Thou sealest up the sum, full of wisdom, and perfect in beauty. Thou hast been in Eden the garden of God; every precious stone was thy covering, the sardius, topaz, and the diamond, the beryl, the onyx, and the jasper, the sapphire, the emerald, and the carbuncle, and gold: the workmanship of thy tabrets and of thy pipes was prepared in thee in the day that thou wast created. Ezekiel 28:11-13 (KJV)

One of the most important things to do in order to know your opponent is to study your opponent. In boxing each boxer is studying their opponent and taking notes on the combinations his/her opponent likes to use the most. Therefore, you will need to study and learn your opponent in life.

Satan, formerly known as Lucifer, doesn't always come dressed down, but most of the time, he's dressed in exactly what you want in a spouse and/or job but later find out that neither of those were meant for you. You must know his attacks and the methods he uses to attack you.

As I matured as a believer and learned more about the Bible; I began to understand that there were a lot of times in my life that satan was attacking me and I didn't know it. I was battling within myself, my thoughts, my actions, and my words; I was having this inward raging war and at the time, I thought I was fighting myself. You see, the devil will even use you against you to confuse and keep you from focusing on God. The sexual assault, the bad relationships, the cutting, and the low self-esteem were schemes created to make me lose my focus. The devil used it to defeat me, but God used it to make me victorious! This is why it's so important to know your creator and your opponent. We have to know when it is the Holy Spirit speaking to us and when it is the devil.

Characteristics of satan.

Ye are of your father the devil, and the lusts of your father ye will do. He was a murderer from the beginning, and abode not in the truth, because there is no truth in him. When he speaketh a lie, he speaketh of his own: for he is a liar, and the father of it.- John 8:44 (KJV)

The devil is a murderer, there is no truth in him, he is

a liar. Proof is in the scripture above! He is the father of lies, so why do we listen to him?

Lucifer was the highest angel, the most beautiful, the wisest, if we had to pick one word, it would be perfection. God created him to be the anointed cherub, most people say he was God's best friend, Ezekiel 28: 11-19, gives a full description of Lucifer, referring to the King of Tyre, speaking to the devil that's behind, King Tyre's madness. Lucifer was full of gemstones such as carnelian, a precious stone, chrysolites, moonstone, beryl, onyx, jasper, sapphire, turquoise, emerald, and gold. He had tabrets all around him, and played the best music in all of heaven, and he walked among the stones of fire. But God said iniquity was found in him; he became violent and sinned, he became proud because of his beauty, and he corrupted his wisdom for splendor.

Lucifer wanted to be higher than God; he wanted to rule the world, but God cast him from heaven and satan became his name.

Studying my opponent has been very interesting. He was the highest angel, the most beautiful, and it still was not enough for him. He wanted more, not only that, he didn't want to do what God created him to do. Some of us know what we are called to do and run away from our purpose as if it is something that could hurt us, your purpose sets you free.

Lucifer became rebellious, evil, cunning, not teachable, and the father of lies. He has been on both sides, good and bad, he knows how to approach us as an ally; then eventually unmasks himself as our adversary. He uses false prophets and apostles to get to the children of God, which is why we have to be on our guard, at all times.

Know your opponent, but also know you!

Who are you? What are your likes and dislikes? What easily tempts you? These are some good things to know when operating everyday because the devil will use your weaknesses against you. He knows them well and he knows your destiny. Eventually you will pick up on the moments when you know it's him trying to deter you and distract you. Don't let him. For example, every time I try to adjust my attitude and say, today, I'm not going to have an attitude, it seems almost immediate that the devil tempts me. It seems so small, but it is so real. We have to pray over those areas where we are weak and ask God to strengthen us. He is our strength in our times of weakness.

From the outside looking in, it may seem as if he has an advantage over you, but he doesn't. If we would tap into our own greatness and our identity in Christ, we would know that the devil may know our destiny, he may know our weaknesses, but he's already defeated because we have the Almighty God fighting on our side.

The Fight

The enemy attacks at any time whether you're sleep or awake. Some of us are being attacked while being asleep and wide awake at the same time. I have had many spiritual encounters and many spiritual dreams, in which were spiritual battles.

One night I fell asleep and in my dream, I was trying to help this little blonde haired girl. I don't know her name or even what I was trying to keep her from but I was holding her hand, and the devil came and tried to snatch her away from me.

He said, "You can't save her, I have you wrapped around my finger."

I woke up in tears and cried out because I was afraid, but I thought about my purpose. I love empowering youth and I have a passion for them. I know that I am to help rise up adolescent girls by teaching them self-confidence and self-love, helping to prevent them from the horrors of my life and what I went through. And it dawned on me that even in my sleep the devil was trying to scare me out of my purpose, but I said NO! Believers, we cannot allow the devil to scare us out of our purpose, or destiny, our reason for living. If we don't survive then somebody doesn't get what they need from God. So I didn't let that dream deter me and I kept pushing, through the pain and the fear of failing.

Another dream consisted of me being caught in the middle of a tornado. Literally! I was floating in the middle of it and it is said that tornadoes are a sign of chaos in a person's life. Well, I was in the middle of one, but I was spit out of the tornado, I survived and went to tell the people about the storm that was coming. God was telling me that even in chaos, I am the messenger to the people; I am the one who has to tell them about the upcoming storm and help get them ready! I love how God allows us to be a vessel for His word and how He trusts us to go tell the others about the gospel! Although the devil will slip into your dreams, God will show up as well.

The last dream I will share with you has happened more recently in the last year or so, my husband and I were at a cabin with a friend of mine and her husband. The guys went outside to do "country boy" things; hunt, or something of that matter. My friend and I were sitting at the table talking and laughing and a bird came down from the sky and started attacking and pecking my ear uncontrollably. It was so hard that in reality, my husband was calling my name, asking if I was okay and when I finally woke up, he said he thought I was having a seizure. At first, I laughed it off and I said it was a bird attacking me in my dream. And my poor husband was a little disturbed and worried as a person should be. But later that week, I spoke to my pastor and minister sister and both stated that it sounded like God was warning me to watch who was in my ear. I prayed about it and got confirmed that there was some negativity around me that needed to be avoided and I prayed it off and it was gone. The bird was so forceful that I know it wasn't a representative of God because He's peaceful and calm. This bird was pecking the life out of my ear. So the devil tried it again, but I won that victory!!

Dreams are crazy and they are not the same for every person. I am not saying that you are going to have the exact same dreams as me or similar experiences but when you begin to get closer to your Lord and Savior, by praying, studying His word and ultimately spending more time with Him. The devil will attack. I can't tell you how he will attack you but just be on guard that he will. Know yourself, know your weaknesses and be on guard for the attacks. Satan has to get permission from God before he can mess with you, (see Job 1:11-12 (KJV)). Therefore, when he comes, understand that God trusts you and He knows He will get the glory out of you. Take pride in that and knock satan out!

Never leave the house without the full armor of God!

Score

Devil- 0

God- 4

Tiera Gandy

Prayer:

Heavenly father, I ask that you will cover this fighter from the crown of his/her head to the soles of his/her feet Lord. I pray that you will teach him/her how to recognize the devil set apart from You, Lord. God have your way in this individual's life and allow him/her to get to know the devil's tactics and be able to withstand the hurt and the pain, the attacks and to cling on to you throughout the storm. I pray that this individual will learn how to simply just call out the name of Jesus and instantly find that the devil MUST flee. That he is commanded to flee. I pray that you allow this person to not be afraid of the devil and his demons but to completely and whole heartedly trust you, which will strengthen his or her faith and instantly be free from the devil's tricks. Lord, we thank you for the trials and tribulations, the hurts and the pains and we know that you are using them ALL for our good. We love you dearly and worship you. In Jesus' Name, we pray,

Amen.

How has the devil attacked you? Identify your weaknesses. (This is where the attacks begin)

_____

_____

_____

_____

_____

_____

_____

_____

_____

_____

_____

_____

Tiera Gandy

_____

_____

_____

_____

_____

_____

_____

_____

_____

_____

_____

_____

Round V:

The Call

For many are called, but few are chosen.

– Matthew 22:14 (KJV)

Tiera Gandy

I have always known I was called to do something great. I felt it even as a child, but simply didn't understand it. It was funny because growing up, people at my parent's church would say there was something special about me. But of course, being a child, we say in our heads: "they say that to everybody."

As a child I battled with wanting everyone to like me, the weird thing is, I always had friends, but for some reason, it felt as if I was the odd one out, everywhere I went. I was the youngest of four by eleven years. I have nieces and nephews closer in age to me than my own brothers and sisters. And very few cousins to grow up with locally. I felt as if I missed out at times, my brothers and sisters had each other, and then there was me.

In high school I was the captain of my basketball team my senior year and I was selected by my teammates. It's funny because, I didn't really know I was a leader but they all looked up to me. Unknowingly, I've been a leader most of my life. I was the bossy child at daycare.

But after analyzing a few things in my life and the things I've been through and the things I have done, I realize that God called me and set me apart, many years before I ever knew anything about what that meant. To be set apart is one of the most beautiful, promising things God could ever do in your life. To be set apart means that God has His hand on you for a specific purpose and throughout my life in different stages and ages, God set me apart to be different for a bigger reason than I could never imagine. God has set you apart as well, for His purpose in your life and it's up to you to answer that call.

I left my family church in 2012, set out to look into other churches, my best friend invited me to her church; a church full of young people on fire for God, and my God it was amazing! I fell in love with the Holy Spirit and the word God planted for me to receive at that church. In 2013, I finally said yes to God and decided to join minister's class and manifest the vision God had for me.

The Fight

During this time of going through the class, the devil was attacking me pretty hard, trying to make me give up and take my focus off of God and all of the youth I was going to touch, but I didn't let him. The devil was trying to discourage and tell me because of my mistakes, I would not be able to minister or change lives, but God said He would use my pain for my purpose.

One day, I was driving home from church, and I had this tremendous amount of pain, heartache, in my heart and in my stomach and I began to cry out loud. I didn't understand what was going on with me, but I called my pastor and asked him,

"What if I'm not good enough? Why do I have this heavy burden to build the young people up?"

It's like I could feel the pain of their very souls in mine, and I couldn't bear all of the pain I was enduring. Pastor walked me through it and he said that I wouldn't know the questions I asked until God brought me to them. There were some things God had to put me through to help get me to that destination. So I took that, and I fought through with prayer and never looked back. God said He could turn my life around just like he did with the woman at the well. So I trusted Him and I pushed through every class and the closer to ordination, the harder it got.

You have to understand that the devil doesn't give up on you when you find God and your purpose for your life in Him. The devil tries harder to make you quit, because he doesn't want you to get to your purpose and enjoy your destiny or the life God created for you, but you have to learn to push through the pain. This is where you endure. You endure the pain, you endure the heartaches, the nights when you are in bed crying and praying out to God, this is your season of endurance, can you out last the devil? It's not easy to push through and fight your own inner demons, staying in when you really want to go out. You have to be prepared and ready to defeat him down on your knees in prayer. You learn how to fight even when you're stumbling and barely hanging on. Persevere, endure, and finish strong.

The great Bishop, prophesied over me, during a very painful time in my life, before ordination. He told me that I was in a spiritual fight and God knew my pain, but was with me every step of the way. He put his hands up as if he were fighting with gloves and said, God said keep fighting, you're learning, you just have to learn how to bob and weave. Here I am, 4 years later writing a book about boxing, The Final Round: Fight for Your Life. God again! I remember it

Tiera Gandy

in my heart, to this day and I have it written down so I don't forget. Be careful who you allow to pray over you but be sure that you remember the authentic pastors, bishops and the prophesies spoken over you, hold on to them, write them down and remember them in your heart. When you get discouraged, remember the prophesy and visions God gave you. They are for YOU!

My minister sisters and I finished minister's class, of the ones who started out, three of us who finished, passed our tests, and the next step was to be ordained. I was so nervous, scared, and anxious all at the same time; I was getting married to God. It was time!

112

At ordination, the greatest feeling was knowing that the Holy Spirit was present and resting on us, as we had our families and close friends there in support. The pastors laid hands on us and it's almost as if you could see the transformation in the spirit realm. It was so powerful. God was most definitely there, front and center.

After the ordination service, Bishop runs up to me and tells me all of these great things that are about to happen in my life, and he prophesied even more greatness into my life. He said in the next five years, things were going to be really great for me and some more things in perfect detail. Well, I'm in my fourth year, no way to go but up! I smiled and cried and accepted all he said. He kept saying, you're going to do great things, I believe in you; you can do it. Keep going, don't quit and he even ran up to my parents giving them the same information, telling them how special I was and that I was going to do great things in my lifetime. Sometimes I get discouraged, and I have to remember what God said. It does not matter what the devil tries to get you to think, what God has said concerning you, is for you. That was an amazing, miraculous day!

Answering the call is not always the call to ministry, but it's ultimately what God has called you to do, for His purpose in your life. Your purpose will not be the same as mine or the person next to you, but our reason for life and being here on earth is for the bigger picture, to build the kingdom of God. It's up to you to search God for it and to ask Him to help you manifest what His vision is for your life.

I answered the call, I followed through, and most importantly, God won my soul!

Will you say YES?

Score

Devil- 0

God- 5

Tiera Gandy

Prayer

Lord we know that you have a purpose for each and every person who was placed on this earth. We know that you when you created us even in our mother's womb, you knew what you would use us for. Lord I ask that you touch this fighter wherever he/she is weak Lord, wherever he/she has questions on what it is he/she is supposed to do, Lord. Help this individual be still and listen for YOUR voice. Help us to only hear your voice, allow our ears to be deaf to the devils tricks but sound to your direction and guidance. God teach us how to operate properly in ministry as we serve our church, teach us how to be true servant leaders, humbled in heart and ready to serve your people. Help us to remember our why in all that we do, to BUILD THE KINGDOM OF GOD. Lord push us past our limits, for we know with you there are no limits God, knock down the walls of fear and allow us to tap into the greatness, you have placed in side of us. Lord, we love you so much and we ask that you would continue to put your hands in our lives and build hedges around us protecting us from the enemy; he might can mess with us, he may even be able to touch us, but he can't kill us! Thank you, Lord for your word and your unconditional love,

In Jesus' Name we pray, Amen.

Have you been called, if not, will you answer when He does? Then what steps will you take to follow Him?

_____

_____

_____

_____

_____

_____

_____

_____

_____

_____

_____

_____

Tiera Gandy

_____

_____

_____

_____

_____

_____

_____

_____

_____

_____

_____

_____

_____

Round VI:

One Flesh

Therefore shall a man leave his father and mother, and be joined to his wife; and they shall become one flesh. —Genesis 2:24 (KJV)

God ordained for a marriage to be between a man and a woman and for the man to leave his mother and father and become one with his wife. Marriage is work and can be challenging at times, but it is so worth the fight to push through and make it each year. I am so grateful that God blessed me to be married to my husband.

I met my husband in October of 2010. It was my first time out with friends in a long time and there he was, at IHOP. We went through a lot in the five years we dated which was off and on, but we made it to the altar. Our story is not perfect, but who's is? It took a lot of work, forgiveness, and unconditional love on both of our parts to get here. But God! In this chapter, I am not going to give you the full details of our journey on how we got here, but I am going to encourage you and help you learn how to push through and pray for your marriage or your future marriage.

Recently, I have seen so many of my close friends and family go through rough times and get divorced on so many issues in which I know no detail of but it breaks my heart that it is happening so frequently. Our marriages are missing the most important piece of the puzzle, God.

I am by no means an expert on marriage, but I encourage you to first be prayerful in your marriage if you aren't already. Specifically, pray with your spouse and watch God change your marriage for the better. Pray for your spouse in areas he/she may be lacking, and pray for yourself so you can meet half way. God must come first in both of your lives, your spouse second, your children, and everything else after that.

I am proud to say that my mother and father have been married for forty-two (42) years! They will tell you, it was not easy and I am sure there were times they wanted to give up, but I thank God that He didn't allow that to happen. If you ask them how they got this far, they would most definitely say the grace of God brought them through. Throughout marriage, you're going to change, as well as your spouse, but it's important for you to allow those changes and to adapt to them and continue to pray and ask God to help you both adjust to the changes.

My husband and I have been married for almost two (2) years, and again, we are clearly still toddlers in this thing, but we have our ups and downs and are still learning each other as husband and wife. Neither one of us have been married before, so we have no idea what we are doing, but we are working together to get it right! Being that we are one as the scripture in the beginning of this chapter said, if he hurts, I hurt and vice versa. Sometimes we get so caught up with life that we may argue over something small that later turns into something big. Couples, we have to be aware that the devil will seep through even the smallest cracks to get a rise out of you. So instead of being at war with each other, we need to be at war with the devil. He's the one we should be fighting.

Therefore, take heed to a few things I have observed and learned in my marriage that I believe will help other newlyweds and maybe even some of you more mature couples!

Tiera Gandy

Pray together. Pray together as a couple for your marriage, your children, your purposes, your careers, and your complete life all together. Add those close to you, and other things you all may need to pray for, such as finances. Ask God what your marriage purpose is!

Pray for one another. Pray for your spouse. Always, always, always pray for your spouse. You would think that every husband and wife would tell the loved one everything but this is not always the case. Some husbands and wives are not always open. You never know what he/she could be going through at work, so keep that prayer line open.

Be selfless. It is so easy to be a selfish spouse.

124

Especially if you're still new at this like myself and my husband. Consider your spouse before you make a decision whether it's to quit your job or to hang out with friends. It simply shows respect toward your spouse.

Study your spouse. This is one of the most romantic, I believe. To study your spouse as if he or she is your favorite subject in school. Learn everything about him or her, by observation, or just by listening and paying attention. For example, your spouse might want to go see a movie that's coming out next week, so maybe you go get tickets and take him or her to see the movie as a surprise date night. Always pay attention to small things such as that and take notes.

Communication is huge. Effective communication is a key factor in all relationships but especially in marriages. Sometimes we can misconstrue what the other is saying, take it the wrong way or simply misread it in a text. One thing that I say all the time and this is for me as well, sometimes it's not what you say but how you say it. So it is very important to be a great communicator and to most definitely learn and understand how your spouse reacts to confrontation. I am a fixer, so I have to fix it right away, whereas, my husband has to take some time to himself and get away from the situation, so we both have to compromise. Sometimes it works and sometimes it doesn't. Like I said, we are toddlers and are still learning.

Learn your spouse's love language. The 5 Love Languages is an awesome book for married couples. I recommend every married couple to read the book together and take the quiz; it is so rewarding and it helps you love your spouse the way he or she expects and wants to be loved.

Fight with your spouse, not against your spouse.
The devil hates marriage and like I said, he will find any small tactic to create a problem in your marriage. Remember that your spouse is your partner, your teammate and you all have to win together. If one of you loses, you both lose, if one of you wins, you both win. When you look at life as you and your spouse against the world, your foundation is strong and you can move forward knowing God is with you. So, when it gets to that point where you feel as if you're going against your teammate, remember, take a step back, pray and keep in mind your goal is to fight for your marriage, not against it.

Tiera Gandy

Shout out to my husband for being my best friend, lover, my headache, but the only person who really knows me and understands me. Thank you for loving me at my best and at my worst, that is most definitely unconditional love. I thank God for you every day!

Date Your Spouse. Plan dates with only you and your spouse. Leave the children with grandma or a sitter, so you all can have some time together. It is very important that you have this alone time. Schedule it out and keep the fire in the dating area of your relationship.

Marriage wins!

Devil- 0

God- 6

<u>Prayer</u>

Lord I pray for the husband/wife reading this chapter. I pray that he/she has the strength to keep going no matter what the struggle is in their marriage. Lord, we know that marriage is hard, and it is not for the weak, but we know that we can be strengthened as couples in our relationship with you, for when three come together, miracles can be made. I pray that you would help each married couple desire to put you first in their marriage and their spouse second, not third behind kids or ministry, but second behind God. I pray that you will teach each couple to pray with each other consistently every day and study Your word together to strengthen their marriage spiritually, for we know the battle is won in the spirit realm. You have proven that anything is possible with You, so teach us how to include you in all our decisions from buying a new car to buying a new home, and to pray for one another and with each other consistently,

In Jesus' name, we pray,

Amen.

If you are already a wife/husband, how can you improve to be a better spouse? Singles, what kind of wife or husband do you want to be?

_____

_____

_____

_____

_____

_____

_____

_____

_____

_____

_____

_____

_____

_____

_____

_____

_____

_____

_____

_____

_____

_____

_____

_____

_____

_____

_____

131

Round VII

The Final Round:

The Knock Out

I therefore so run, not as uncertainly; so fight I, not as one that beateth the air: - 1Cor 9:26 (KJV)

It is time! Your fight either ends or begins right now. Picture this; you are in the locker room- your prayer room, getting ready for the fight of the day, God is back there with you. He's listening to your concerns about this fight, and in return, He's telling you that you are going to win. It is already done, fighter. All you have to do is show up for the fight.

Next is your announcement--the call, introducing, the greatest, strongest fighter alive!!!! God is calling you to the ring! As you come out of the locker room, the crowd- his angels are rooting for you! Fighter, this is your time and the time is now. As you walk into the ring and the music is playing, the angels are cheering and God is your coach in the corner.

Preparing you for the fight, God then whispers, "the fight is fixed, I set you up." Believers and unbelievers, when you realize that God uses absolutely everything that happens to you for your good and turns it into a masterpiece, you won't worry about the next round, because you will be convinced that you've already won.

No matter what level you're on or what round you are in, God is there coaching you. He is in your corner yelling for you, telling you when to bob and weave, to watch out for what the devil is trying to throw at you and He's pleading for you not to give up. People we cannot give up in this fight, our role, and our purpose is to outlast our opponent.

Every fight you've ever had has been preparing you for right now. The devil is afraid of you. He does not want you to find your purpose or to know who you are in Christ which is why he attacks our minds! The devil did not want me to finish this book because he knows the effect it will have on people. He knows that I am going to talk about Jesus and how He saved me from myself and I am going to do whatever it takes to empower the next person to become a believer and to trust God. It does not get easier, but it's not supposed to.

So what are you going to do about it? Are you going to give in to the devil and allow him to continue to control your life and tell you what to believe about yourself and convince you that you are not enough?

Stay alert!

The fight of your life is not only for your

survival, but it's for the survival of your children, your friends, your family, your wife, husband, and your purpose. Let me put it into perspective for you. I tried to commit suicide at age fifteen (15). I am currently thirty (30) years old, had I committed suicide fifteen (15) years ago, first of all, I would not be writing this book. Second, I would not have married my husband nor had the opportunity to become a mother. Lastly, I would have not made the difference I've made in so many lives, including girls and young women who have been sexually assaulted or molested, not healed, men and women in search for Christ and their purpose. I wouldn't have become this inspiring, motivational human being. I would have only been a long lost teenager who thought it could never get better. But thank God for my mother who saved my life, my angel. I have made a difference in the world and community around me and plan to do so much more, if God permits it.

The fight for your life begins in your mind. Our minds are like sponges, and they absorb every thought whether it's positive or negative, but it's all about what you feed yourself. If you feed negativity to yourself, you will be negative and vice versa. Be careful of your thoughts; they can and will take over you if you don't take control of them.

The devil will throw everything at you to encourage you to give up but there's one maybe a few reasons why you can't: Your Why!

As I get ready to close out this book, my first book, before we pray I want to ask you a question:

Tiera Gandy

What is your why? Or a better question who is your why? What is your reason for getting up every morning to go to work or school to better your education or to get a check every two weeks or month? Why do you do it? Is it just for the fun of it or is there a purpose behind it?

I was talking to my Charm School 101 girls about public speaking; they were learning to speak in front of people. So I allowed them to listen to one of my favorite motivational speakers. On this particular video, he was talking about dropout prevention for students in high school. He was a high school dropout, and he went to a conference to speak to administrators, teachers, and other school leaders. He told his audience to find out what their students' why is. He told them to stop telling the students that they should stay in school or continue in education after high school, simply because they will make money. He said ask them who they are doing this for. So as my girls were listening to the videos, one of them got a little emotional, and she said he's right, teachers always tell us to stay in school so we can make money, but the speaker advised the administrators and teachers to post pictures of the students' why's around the classrooms, their grandmother, their mother, their father, and/or guardians, and see how things change in the classroom. So I told them my why; my why is first God, my husband, my son and daughter, charm school 101 girls, the women connected to me, and every stranger God places in my path to speak to, my why is YOU. It is bigger than money, my why are people I love dearly whom I would lay it on the line for. Can you say you would die for your why?

So I ask you:

Who is your why? _____

Why did you select that person? _____

_____

_____

_____

_____

_____

_____

_____

_____

The Final Round: Fight for Your Life

If God came down right now and asked if you'd

say yes; would you?

Yes or No

If you are still breathing, the fight ain't over!

Keep fighting!

Score

Devil- 0

God- 7

THE FIGHT IS FIXED!

Tiera Gandy

Prayer

Lord, first of all thank you God, for allowing me to finish this book, You know what it took for me to get through this and finish. You've been with me every step of the way. Not wanting to write, being afraid to challenge the devil with this book, but you said that the people needed it. So Lord, thank you for pushing me, for giving me a husband to push me and encourage me and family and friends who have been there holding me accountable. God I want to lift up this fighter right now, thank you for this individual who decided to pick this book up and read our story Lord. I pray that it has touched him/her and that it has encouraged them to fight for their lives, their souls. During the knock out, we have found that all we have to do is stand, and outlast our opponent, the devil. We have learned that the fight is in the word of God, in prayer and in fasting. God, I ask that you would help us learn how to do all three however you want us to do it. Help us to study your word, help us to pray daily and to fast when you call us to fast. We want to live our lives for you, Lord. If we don't have anybody else to do this for, we most definitely do it for you. God thank you for being here, for helping us to understand you better. God help us through each and every battle that will come in the future, the obstacles that will try to trip us up and even the distractions we sometimes cause ourselves. We trust you Lord, and we give our lives to you Lord. We love you, we cherish you, and we adore you. In Jesus' name, we pray, Amen.

Write out your strategy on how you will knock your opponent out. What are some things you can start doing today to win in the final round?

_____

_____

_____

_____

_____

_____

_____

_____

_____

_____

_____

_____

_____

Tiera Gandy

_____

_____

_____

_____

_____

_____

_____

_____

_____

_____

_____

_____

_____

Bonus Chapter:

FREEDOM

1 There is therefore now no condemnation to them which are in Christ Jesus, who walk not after the flesh, but after the Spirit.
2 For the law of the Spirit of life in Christ Jesus hath made me free from the law of sin and death.

Romans 8:1-2 (KJV)

In Jesus Christ, you are free. The people of God will win! The fight is fixed! He came down here so we could live. He died so we could live. God gave his only begotten son so we could have life. Not only that, after Jesus died, God left us a comforter in the Holy Spirit. God cares about us so much, and He wants us to know that we are not alone and that we are free because of Jesus.

There are so many people I know who are falling away from Christ and the Bible and it breaks my heart. But the bible said it would be this way in the last days. Personally, I have a heart to serve and help people come to Christ and when I see them falling away, I feel responsible. What I have come to realize is that we can't save everyone. But the good news is, we can try.

So fighter, as I stated before, the fight is fixed! You do not have to stay bound to that broken relationship, the negative mentality, or to the cancer you are fighting against. You have already won! God just wants you to know that through Jesus Christ you are free and as long as you have Him, your opponent is defeated. But it's up to you if you want to win the fight. You can walk away from your chains whenever God permits you to. Some of us are like caged birds. We have come to be comfortable in our space, confined to just the four faces of the cage and nothing else. God has even opened the door for us and we stay right where we are, content with mediocrity because we don't know we have the freedom to fly. We are bound by our mistakes, our insecurities and most of all by fear. We act as if we don't deserve to be liberated or free, so we continue to wallow in our self-pity and remain chained to the things God is trying to deliver us from. God did not call you to sit in a cage or a box. He called you to go out into the world and make a difference. He called you to use your testimony to grow and to help people you come in contact with.

Confession, I was afraid to write this book and to be honest I am fearful of finishing it. It feels as if I have this heavy burden on my shoulders that won't be lifted until I publish this book. God has already given me my next writing assignment, but I can't start on it because I have been afraid to finish this one. Sometimes we block our own blessings by taking too long on a project God told us to finish a year ago. We must be obedient and do as He says or we might miss out on a great opportunity.

We also have to let go of our fears and get rid of our excuses and jump off the edge of the cliff. Understand, God will help you fly, but you have to let go of whatever it is you are trying to hold on to. God has been speaking to me in my dreams and He has made it very clear that I have to trust Him and to make it simple, JUST JUMP. I've already won because the fight is fixed. I don't have to worry, because God said it!

You know what it feels like to be free? No more heavy burdens, no more pain, you are free. Jesus came to earth to show us a perfect way to live. Although we are not perfect, He was. He lived a sin free life and came only to fulfill his purpose. Don't get me wrong, He felt human emotions and even wanted to stay, but

He quickly said, not my will but thine, be done.

Saying, Father, if thou be willing, remove this cup from me: nevertheless not my will, but thine, be done. Luke 22:42 (KJV)

You may be struggling with your purpose and you may feel God tugging at your heart, just remember, not your will, but His will, be done. God is going to get the glory out of you either way willingly or not. But there is freedom in walking in your purpose that God has provided for you. Will you be attacked? Yes, but you will have the weapons needed for every attack on every level that the devil tries to destroy.

Trust Him and His will for your life and live

your life out loud.

You've already won! The Fight is FIXED! Live out your purpose and allow God to have control of your life and watch Him do a work in you!

The Final Round is coming, the world will be at war and people will fall away from the truth. You have a job to do, you have a purpose to fulfill, and there are people who are connected to you who are counting on you to survive. Keep fighting!

Fight until the final round, it aint over until the trumpets sound!!! Listen to His commands and remember you can do ALL things! Never forget that!

Philippians 4:13 (KJV)

If I died today, I would have left my mark.

What about you?

Tiera Gandy

Prayer

Heavenly father, I pray that you would help and show this fighter that not only is the fight fixed, but you have been there and will be there by his or her side, in the long run. Help he/she understand that you will never leave them. We pray that you would show them freedom in their purpose. Help them to discern the enemies attacks and to know what weapons to use. Lord, we love you and are so grateful that you sent your son to die so we could be free. We ask that you would forgive us of our sins and help us to not make the same mistakes, but to learn from. We also ask that you would help us learn to tell our testimonies when you see fit, to help the unbelievers and believers around us. We ask that you not exempt anyone, Lord. We thank you for your constant unconditional love and for allowing us to see another day. We love you wholeheartedly,

In Jesus' name, we pray,

Amen

Are you saved?

Yes   or   No

If not, please see below:

That if thou shalt confess with thy mouth the Lord Jesus, and shalt believe in thine heart that God hath raised him from the dead, thou shalt be saved. Romans 10:9 (KJV)

God says if you confess with your mouth that Jesus is Lord and believe in your heart that he died and was raised from the dead, and you will be saved.

Say this with me:

Lord, I confess my sins to you and I turn away from them; I believe that you are the one and only, Lord Jesus Christ, who died on the cross for me and my sins, and was raised from the dead so that I could live. Thank you, Lord, for your sacrifice and for your perfect will and obedience, I love you, I worship you, and I lift you up. In Jesus Name, I Pray, Amen.

That's it, you're saved.

Heavenly Father.,

God thank you so much for providing the vision, allowing the storms to come, all so I could be a blessing to your will for my life. I pray that this book will touch the people it needs to touch and that it will light the way for those who are lost. God I love you more than anything in this world, and I don't have the words to express my gratitude, all I can do is praise you and worship you. You are amazing, and I thank you that you saw fit for me to fulfill this journey. I love you so much, and I am forever grateful to be walking in purpose and in Your will for my life!

I love you!

Your servant daughter,

Tiera Gandy

Follow us on Facebook and Instagram:

FB: The Final Round: Fight for Your Life

IG: thefinalroundffyl

Booking: thefinalroundKO@outlook.com

Offering: Motivational speaking, ministering, life coaching, and workshops.